Monsieur ARMAND

Written by Judith A. Martin

Illustrated by Greg Holfeld

ETA Cuisenaire

Monsieur Armand
ISBN 0-7406-1011-2
ETA 351061

Revised American edition published in 2004 by ETA/Cuisenaire®
under license from Era Publications. All rights reserved.

Text © Judith A. Martin
Illustrations © Greg Holfeld

ETA/Cuisenaire Product Development Manager: Mary Watanabe
Lead Editor: Betty Hey
Editorial Team: Kevin Anderson, Kim O'Brien, Nancy Sheldon,
  Elizabeth Sycamore
Educational Consultant: Geraldine Haggard, Ed.D.

ETA/Cuisenaire • Vernon Hills, IL 60061-1862
800-445-5985 • www.etacuisenaire.com

Printed in China.

04 05 06 07 08 09 10 11 12 13   10 9 8 7 6 5 4 3 2 1

Table of Contents

Chapter 1

Monsieur Armand had run out of
patience. He threw open the kitchen
window of the restaurant.

"For the last time — go away, goose!"
he yelled. "How can I work with all of
your honking?"

The goose was in the farmyard
next door. It looked up from
where it was feasting on the wild
gooseberries that grew along the
restaurant fence. But at Monsieur
Armand's words, it only
honked louder.

The chef tore off his apron.
His face grew very red —
as red as the beets he
was preparing for his
favorite soup.

"Why don't you go and bother
someone else for a change?"
he asked. "You are giving me
a pain in my neck."

But, the goose was very
stubborn. It would
not move.

"You … you!" stammered Monsieur Armand. Without thinking, he grabbed the closest thing — the saucepan full of his beloved soup — and threw it out the window at the goose.

Whoosh, splat!
Honk, honk!

The goose flapped its wings,
but stayed where it was. The
soup lay splattered all over the
grass. Ruined!

Monsieur Armand pulled off his chef's cap and threw it on the floor. He flipped his lid.

"My soup, my soup!" he cried. "You have ruined my soup! Now what will I serve the customers?"

He grabbed a large kitchen knife and leaned out the window, swinging in all directions. Whip, whip, whip went the air.

The goose got such a fright that it flew away at once. It hissed and honked clear across the farmyard.

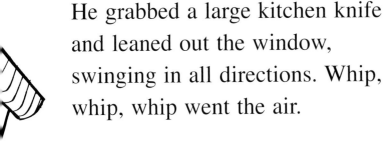

14

"Good-for-nothing goose!" called Monsieur Armand after it. "If I ever catch you …" His eyes fell on the knife. An interesting idea came to him. He raised one eyebrow menacingly.

"Maybe … NOT so good-for-nothing after all."

Later that morning, painters arrived
at the restaurant and started working.
They made a sign advertising an exotic
new dish on the menu — GOOSE.

Chapter 2

That night, when the restaurant had closed, Monsieur Armand changed into a long black coat, gloves, and a beret. He slipped a flashlight into the pocket of his pants and tucked a large cloth sack inside his jacket. Then he covered his entire face with dark chocolate icing.

"Now, Madame Goose,"
he announced, licking
his lips, "I am ready
for you!"

Under the cover of darkness, he slipped out of the restaurant and into the gooseberry bushes. All was quiet on the farm. The animals were safely shut away in the barn for the night.

Monsieur Armand tiptoed across the farmyard. Unfortunately, the night was very dark and his flashlight gave off only a dull beam of light. He had not gone very far when he tiptoed straight into a sloppy, smelly, messy cow flop.

He muttered and complained,
"Just you wait, goose!"

The barn door creaked as he slipped around it. Inside, the smell was overwhelming. Monsieur Armand held his nose as he shone his flashlight around.

He could see the animals in their stalls. At the very back of the barn, nesting on some straw, was the goose. Near the goose, he saw what looked like a large sack.

"Lucky me," he chuckled. "Just the place to hide." With that, he crept over and crouched behind it.

Unluckily, the "sack" wasn't a sack after all, but a huge sow, lying down with her piglets.

And hearing a noise behind her, the sow rolled over — right on top of Monsieur Armand.

He was pinned to the ground.

27

The piglets sniffed around him and grunted.

"Shoo, shoo! Go away, little piggies," he wheezed. But too late! They had discovered the delicious chocolate icing camouflaging his face.

Their wet snouts nuzzled his skin.
Their sloppy tongues licked his entire
face.

"Aaaaaargh!" screamed
Monsieur Armand.

Chapter 3

The barn came to life at once. The sow stood up, squealing loudly. Other animals mooed and brayed and hissed and neighed and stomped in their stalls with fright.

Over near the farmhouse, the dogs began to bark, and the farmhouse lights came on.

Monsieur Armand jumped up, his heart pounding. With a mighty tug, he pulled out his sack and ran after the goose.

But the goose saw him coming.

With its beak open,
it flew toward him.
Hissing fiercely, it latched
onto his trousers.

Monsieur Armand turned and ran.
The goose ran after him, still attached.

He ran out of the barn and across the farmyard, until he reached the gooseberry bushes near the restaurant fence. He dived into them for cover.

The goose dived in after him.

Feathers flew from the bushes as Monsieur Armand wrestled with the goose, his hands clutching it tightly.

The goose fixed its stare on Monsieur Armand's nose. A fierce battle erupted. Then, quite suddenly, the farmyard was still again.

Minutes went by before Monsieur
Armand stole back over the restaurant
fence, the bulging sack tucked carefully
under his arm. The farmer, reaching
the scene, could only wonder what had
happened.

Chapter 4

A new day dawned cheerfully at
Monsieur Armand's restaurant. When
the restaurant opened, customers came
in droves to sample his exotic new dish.

The menu board, with a hastily
scribbled addition, announced brightly
— WILD GOOSEBERRY TART.

Monsieur
Armand's

TODAY'S SPECIAL
wild
GOOSE
-berry
tart

Monsieur Armand beamed with pride.
Even the noise of the goose outside
the window didn't bother him on
this day. His fruit tarts were a huge
success. The customers loved them.

The tarts looked magnificent, he agreed. Only it was a shame he couldn't smell them with his nose all bandaged up from the goose's final attack.

"You may have won the battle, goose," he called, as he poured more of the wild gooseberry mixture into the tarts, "but I have won the war!"

Monsieur Armand was a very happy man — well, happy as long as the gooseberries lasted.

The End